ANXIETY
AND
SELF-ESTEEM

HONOR HEAD

W
FRANKLIN WATTS
LONDON • SYDNEY

Franklin Watts
First published in Great Britain in 2020
by The Watts Publishing Group
Copyright © The Watts Publishing Group, 2020

Editor: Amy Pimperton
Designers: Peter Scoulding and Cathryn Gilbert
Cover design: Peter Scoulding
Consultant: Clare Arnold, psychotherapist with 25 years'
experience working with CAMHS, the NHS's Child and
Adolescent Mental Health Services

HB ISBN: 978 1 4451 7216 3
PB ISBN: 978 1 4451 7263 7

Printed and bound in Dubai

Picture credits:
Shutterstock: Nate Allred 7b; Anouki 17c, 30c; BMJ 5tr;
Blanscape 11b; Tatyana Bolotova 22b; Edwin Butter 2,
8t; Mircea Costina 27tr; Gorken Demir front cover, title
page; Deny 21c; fantom_rd 7t; Florida stock 22t; Giedriius
19c; Dmitrii Golubev 24b; Pascale Gueret 23cl; Mario_
Hoppmann 13b; Issumi1 11t, 30b; Kamonrat 13t; KarlDesign
29b; Heiko Kiera 21t; Grigorita Ko 5b, 25r, 30t; Tomas
Kotouc 27b; Kungverylucky back cover, 6; Christopher P
Mcleod 10; David Martinez Moreno 9b; Einar Muoni 24t;
Ivanova N 15t; Nwdph 12;Otsphoto 28; Pakhnyushchy 26;
Nathan Pang 19b; Ondrej Prosicky 8b, 13c, 25cl; Enrique
Ramos 17b; Reikus 4; Slowmotiongli 17t; Adam Van
Spronsen 14; stock_shot 27tl; Johan Swanepoel 11c; Mari
Swanwpoel 29c; David TB 5tl; Alexi TM 15b; Topten22photo
21b; Anna Utekhina 20; ValSN 9t; Michael Verbeek 15c;
Artem Verkhoglyad 18;Vladsilver 7c; John Michael Vosloo
16; Y F Wong 29t; Wynian 23cr; Jimmy Yan 19t.

Franklin Watts, an imprint of
Hachette Children's Group
Carmelite House
50 Victoria Embankment
London EC4Y 0DZ

An Hachette UK Company
www.hachette.co.uk
www.franklinwatts.co.uk

Contents

Everyone faces challenging times in their life. This book will help you to develop the resilience skills you need to cope with difficult situations in all areas of life.

What does it mean to build resilience?

When we build resilience we can better cope with things, such as being bullied or losing a friend. Building resilience means we accept that times are difficult now, but that we can and will get back to enjoying life. Learning how to build resilience is a valuable life skill.

What is a trusted adult?

A trusted adult is anyone that you trust and who makes you feel safe. It can be a parent or carer, a relative or a teacher. If you have no one you want to talk to, phone a helpline (see page 32).

What is anxiety?

Anxiety is feeling scared and worried because we don't know what might happen in the future. We could feel anxious about something like meeting new people, being in the dark, trying something new or even things such as climate change.

Everyone feels anxious sometimes – even grown-ups.

Anxiety can make us very stressed and this can make us feel ill.

When we feel frightened (even when there is nothing to be scared of), when we cannot sleep or start having bad dreams, these could be signs of anxiety.

If you are so anxious about something that it stops you from enjoying yourself, you should talk to someone you trust about how you feel.

What is self-esteem?

Self-esteem is what you feel about yourself. High self-esteem is being happy about who you are. Low self-esteem is feeling that you are not good enough or cannot do anything right.

High self-esteem means we like who we are and enjoy being with other people.

To have high self-esteem does not mean we have to be perfect or good at everything. No one is perfect or good at everything.

As you grow up you will learn more about who you are. You will learn what you like to do, what you are best at and things you are not so good at.

Being proud of who you are will help you to build resilience or bounce back when things go wrong. Think about what you like about being you, such as making people laugh or being helpful at home.

7

Talk about it

You should always talk to a trusted adult if you feel anxious or scared. Talking is a great way to help you sort out problems. It also makes you feel in control.

Feelings and thoughts that make you feel angry, scared or anxious are nothing to be ashamed of. The best way to deal with them is to talk to someone.

Feeling anxious that you might not be collected after school? Have the name and contact details of someone you can phone if this happens.

When you have a sleepover with a friend, call a parent or carer at a set time during the evening. If you feel upset or want to go home, they can collect you or reassure you.

Having a plan makes you feel in control and this can stop you feeling anxious. And if you do feel anxious, you know you can do something about it.

Try new things

Trying new things is exciting, but sometimes we worry that we might fail or not do something well enough. Sometimes we don't try new things because we don't want to disappoint our family, friends or teachers.

Unless you try something new you will never know if you can do it or not.

The most important thing is that you try something new and do your best. Trying is more important than whether you get it right or not.

Be proud that you tried something new even if it didn't work out. Everyone gets things wrong — even grown-ups! This is part of learning to build resilience.

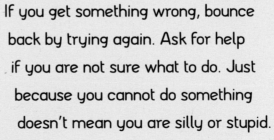

If you get something wrong, bounce back by trying again. Ask for help if you are not sure what to do. Just because you cannot do something doesn't mean you are silly or stupid.

Build your confidence

It is normal to feel anxious when we think we can't do anything right or will mess things up. We think this way because we have no confidence. Having confidence in yourself means you believe that you can do something.

Instead of thinking things might go wrong, think about how well they might go.

To help build up your confidence, set yourself some realistic goals. Make a list of things you would like to achieve, such as writing a poem, trying a new hobby or keeping your room tidy.

At the end of each day think of all the good things you did that day. It can be helping with the chores at home, reading, learning something new at school or talking to a new classmate.

Praise others when they do things well. It makes us feel good when we make others feel happy.

Be yourself

Sometimes we feel bad if a brother or sister, friend or classmate is really good at something and we aren't. It can make you feel like giving up. You should not compare yourself with others.

Not all of us will be good at the same thing.

Just because someone you know is really good at something, this doesn't mean you have to be good at it, too. It would be very boring if we were all great at the same thing.

Everyone has different things they are good at. Focus on what you are doing and be proud that you are doing it as well as you can.

Think about the things that you really love doing and then work towards being the best at them that you can be. For example, if you like swimming, try learning different strokes.

Control your worries

We need to learn to control our worries rather than letting our worries control us. When you start to worry, try doing something else to take your mind off the worry, such as reading a book or listening to music.

Try not to let worrying stop you enjoying yourself and having fun.

Often, when worries are written down, they don't look so bad. Write down or draw your worries and put them in a jar or a box with a lid.

Set aside a 'worry time' for about 10 minutes every day (about an hour before bedtime is perfect). Sit down with an adult, open the worry jar and talk about the worries inside.

After talking about a worry, tear the paper into lots of little pieces and then throw them away. This will help you to let go of your worries and build your resilience.

Be an optimist

An optimist believes that good things will happen. If you are an optimist you expect the best things to happen in any situation. For example, you believe you will make new friends, do well in your test and win the sports match!

Optimists look forward to trying new things and meeting new people.

Being optimistic means that when you try something new you will feel less anxious about it.

If you are an optimist and something fails, you are more likely to bounce back and have another go, rather than giving up.

To help you think like an optimist, at the end of each day think of all the good and fun things that happened that day. Think of three things that you have to look forward to tomorrow.

Accept criticism

Criticism is when you are told you have done something wrong or not well. Everyone at all ages has to learn to accept criticism. The better our self-esteem, the better we can handle criticism.

When someone criticises you it is not because they think you are a bad person, but to help you to learn. Bounce back by believing you can do better and use the criticism to improve.

Criticism should be a good thing.

If you don't understand why someone is criticising you, say so in a polite way. If criticism makes you feel anxious or stressed, talk to the person about how you feel.

If someone makes you feel embarrassed, stupid or silly this is a form of bullying. Tell someone you trust about it.

Make friends

Friends are very important. They can help us to feel good about ourselves. They are people we trust and can have fun with. Friends will also share our problems and help us when we feel anxious.

If you feel anxious about making friends, think of all the lovely things about yourself that would make you a good friend.

Not everyone will get on. This does not mean there is a problem with you, that is just the way it is. You can't be friends with everyone.

Even if you can't be friends, be polite and smile. Don't feel you have to change to fit in with other people.

If your anxiety is stopping you making new friends, talk to someone you trust about it. You shouldn't feel embarrassed, not everyone can make friends easily.

Eat right and exercise

Eating the right food, getting enough exercise and having a good night's sleep all help to make us feel less anxious. Good food and exercise give us the energy to bounce back when things go wrong.

Sleep helps your mind and body to feel happy and healthy.

Try not to eat too many sugary or fatty foods, such as sweets, cakes and crisps. These can make you feel tired, grumpy and anxious.

You should eat to stay happy and healthy, not to change the way you look. Eat fresh fruit and vegetables, brown rice and brown bread, and drink lots of water.

Do some exercise every day. Look for fun games and exercises to try, such as swimming or gymnastics.

Love being you

You are special. There is no one else like you in the whole world! Be proud of who you are, how you look and the things that you do every day.

Be the best person you can be by being kind, polite and honest – and enjoy being you!

We are all different shapes and sizes. Think about how amazing your body is and be proud of it.

Be yourself. If you start to think you want to look or be like someone else, stop. Instead, list all the things you like about yourself.

Choose friends who make you feel good about yourself and who are there for you, even when things go wrong. Good friends will always help you to build resilience.

29

Be resilient!

Being resilient means being able to cope with times when you feel sad or are going through a situation that makes you feel anxious. Here are some things you can do to boost your self-esteem and feel less anxious.

- Start each day with a positive thought. Believe that today will be a good day.

- Take a few minutes to yourself and say something like: 'I can do this' or 'This will be alright', a few times. Take a deep breath and smile.

- Think about a time when you felt confident or proud of what you did. Remember how good you felt and try to keep this feeling.

- When you feel anxious your breathing becomes shallow. Breathe in for a count of three, as if you are smelling a flower. Then breathe out for a count of three. Do this until your breathing is normal again.

- Give your anxiety a name and a face. So, if you are anxious about meeting new people, think of how that worry would look as a person. When the worry starts, face it and tell it to go away and leave you alone.

Notes for parents, carers and teachers

There are many ways parents, carers and teachers can help children develop resilience skills through teaching them how to deal with their anxieties.

Children with low self-esteem find it difficult to accept praise or criticism, are reluctant to try new things, are negative about themselves and give up easily.

Children with anxiety can develop phobias, be very clingy, have separation issues, and may worry that bad things might happen to them, their family or friends. Anxious children may become withdrawn, have panic attacks and tantrums, have trouble sleeping and stomach pains.

Never dismiss a child's anxiety or low self-esteem as being silly or trivial. Try to get them to talk about how they feel and why they feel that way. At home or school, read through this book together. Talk about each scenario.

At school, have a safe, calm space where a child can go at a certain time to talk to someone about bad, worrying or scary feelings, or just to sit and practise deep breathing.

Have an assembly on anxiety and self-esteem. Be clear that these things are common and that everyone, even adults, feel this way at times.

At home, reassure your child that anxiety will pass. Acknowledge how they feel, talk about it and it will seem less scary. Tell children you love them and give them cuddles. Knowing they are loved unconditionally is a big factor in boosting resilience in children.

For children with low self-esteem, encourage and help them to try new things. Be clear that getting it wrong is not a bad thing. Praise their effort. Help them to set goals. Talk about their achievements.

When a child does something wrong, look for positives rather than dwelling on the negatives. Encourage them to try again.

Glossary

anxious feeling worried or scared about how something is going to turn out

ashamed feeling embarrassed or guilty

confidence the belief that you can do something well

disappoint when you do not do as well as someone had hoped

embarrassed feeling uncomfortable or shy

goals things you want to do, such as learning to swim

optimist someone who is hopeful and confident

resilience being able to bounce back from something bad that has happened

self-esteem the way you feel about yourself

shallow not very deep

stressed feeling tense and emotional

Websites

If you need advice or someone to talk to, try these helplines or visit these websites.

For children:
www.childline.org.uk and the 24-hour children's helpline is: 0800 1111
www.kidshealth.org/en/kids/self-esteem.html#catemotion is a good resource for self-esteem and how to improve it.
www.youngminds.org.uk has advice on mental and emotional anxieties.

For adults:
These two sites have advice on how to help children with low self-esteem.
www.kidshealth.org/en/parents/self-esteem.html

www.youngminds.org.uk/find-help/for-parents/parents-guide-to-support-a-z/parents-guide-to-support-self-esteem
(the Young Minds parents' helpline is: 0808 802 5544)

These two sites have advice on how to help anxious children.
www.youngminds.org.uk/find-help/for-parents/parents-guide-to-support-a-z/parents-guide-to-support-anxiety

www.nhs.uk/conditions/stress-anxiety-depression/anxiety-in-children

Index